# CONNECTICUT

## Past and Present

Laura La Bella

rosen publishing's
rosen central®

New York

Published in 2011 by The Rosen Publishing Group, Inc.
29 East 21st Street, New York, NY 10010

Copyright © 2011 by The Rosen Publishing Group, Inc.

First Edition

**Library of Congress Cataloging-in-Publication Data**

La Bella, Laura.
Connecticut: past and present / Laura La Bella. — 1st ed.
   p. cm. — (The United States: past and present)
Includes bibliographical references and index.
ISBN 978-1-4358-9478-5 (library binding)
ISBN 978-1-4358-9505-8 (pbk.)
ISBN 978-1-4358-9539-3 (6-pack)
1. Connecticut—Juvenile literature. I. Title.
F94.3.L325 2011
974.6—dc22

2010000401

*Manufactured in Malaysia*

CPSIA Compliance Information: Batch #S10YA: For further information, contact Rosen Publishing, New York, New York, at 1-800-237-9932.

**On the cover:** Top left: Osborn Hall at Yale University. Top right: A lighthouse at Mystic Seaport. Bottom: The skyline of Hartford.

# Contents

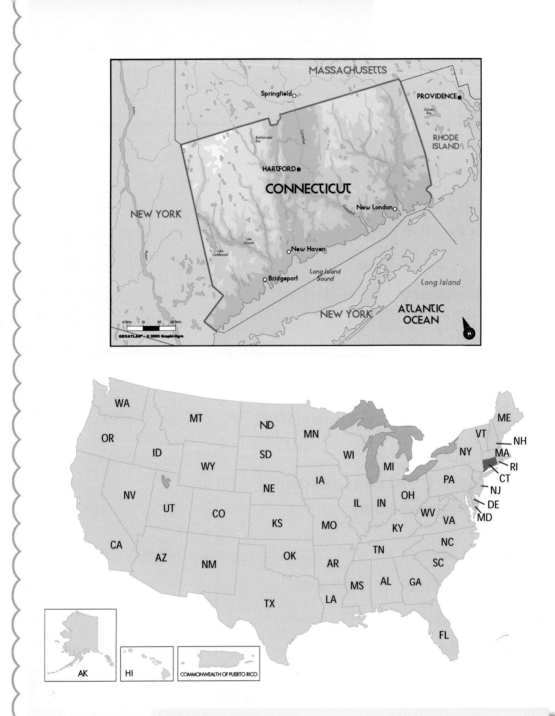

Located on the East Coast, Connecticut borders the states of New York, Massachusetts, and Rhode Island, as well as Long Island Sound, a waterway leading to the Atlantic Ocean.

# Introduction

New England, a cluster of six states, is anchored by one of the oldest states in the country, a state rich in history and with a deep appreciation for ingenuity and innovation. Welcome to Connecticut!

As one of America's oldest states, Connecticut has a long and fascinating history. Part of its history results from its unique location. The Constitution State forms one of the three corners that make up one of the world's most populated areas. The Tri-State area, which includes parts of Connecticut, New York City and its suburbs, and New Jersey, is home to more than twenty-two million people. A majority of southern Connecticut's residents commute daily to New York City for work. Its location also makes it a perfect entry point for travel in New England. Bordered by Rhode Island, Massachusetts, and New York, Connecticut is a gateway to exciting cities such as New York City, Boston, and Providence.

Connecticut boasts far more than its location between other states' attractions and population centers, however. Its largest cities—Bridgeport, Stamford, New Haven, and Hartford—are centers of industry in their own right. They also offer exciting options for exploring history, enjoying the performing arts, and visiting world-class museums and galleries. More than merely a gateway to other destinations or a small part of a larger region, Connecticut is a destination in itself, rich in history, culture, commerce, and natural beauty.

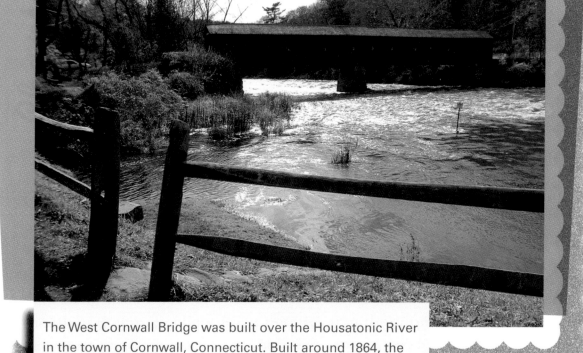

The West Cornwall Bridge was built over the Housatonic River in the town of Cornwall, Connecticut. Built around 1864, the bridge is listed on the National Register of Historic Places.

## Rivers

Connecticut features two significant rivers: the Connecticut River and the Housatonic River. The Connecticut River cuts through the center of the state. At 407 miles (655 kilometers) long, it is the largest river in New England. It flows south from the Connecticut Lakes in northern New Hampshire, through western Massachusetts and central Connecticut, all the way to Long Island Sound, where it empties into the Atlantic Ocean. The Connecticut River is a fresh-water river. The Housatonic River flows south to southeast in western

Massachusetts and western Connecticut. The river is 149 miles (240 km) long, and its mouth is located at Long Island Sound as well.

## Land Regions

The state of Connecticut is divided into five distinct geographic land regions. They are the Taconic Section, the Western New England Upland, the Connecticut Valley Lowland, the Eastern New England Upland, and the Coastal Lowlands.

The Taconic Mountains, or Taconic Range, are found in the northwestern corner of the state. *Taconic* is a Native American word meaning "in the trees." The highest peak in Connecticut is atop Bear Mountain. The mountain is 2,326 feet (709 meters) tall. While it might be the highest peak, it is not the highest point in the state. Mount Frissell enjoys that distinction, at 2,379 feet (725 m) tall. It is a prominent peak of the Taconic Range, part of the Appalachian Mountains. The Taconic Range runs along the eastern border of New York State, and from northwest Connecticut to western Massachusetts.

Most of western Connecticut is part of the region called the Western New England Upland. Steep hills, ridges, and rivers characterize this part of the state. The Upland runs into parts of Massachusetts and Vermont. It gradually descends from northwest to southeast. Its elevation above sea level falls from about 1,400 to 1,000 feet (427 to 305 m) as it descends.

Running through the center of Connecticut and north into Massachusetts is the Connecticut Valley Lowland. This river valley extends north into Massachusetts and is about 30 miles (48 km) wide.

Considerably lower than the Western New England Upland are the river valleys and low hills of the Eastern New England Upland.

# Candlewood Lake

Candlewood Lake is the largest lake in Connecticut, with a surface area of 8.4 square miles (21.8 square kilometers). It also has 86 miles (138 km) of shoreline. Yet this impressive body of water is less than one hundred years old. Under its waters lie what was once rich farmland and countryside settlements in the Rocky River basin, an area surrounded by the towns of Brookfield, New Fairfield, New Milford, Sherman, and Danbury.

In 1917, a lawyer named J. Henry Roraback began buying sites along the Connecticut and Housatonic rivers. He wanted to place dams along these sites to help generate electrical power. After building a dam on the Housatonic River at Derby, Roraback needed to construct a water storage reservoir and a generating station in order to begin generating electricity.

To create this reservoir, the electricity company seized control over the farmland and settlements of the Rocky River basin, a total area of 5,420 acres (2,193 hectares). This land contained churches, schools, farms, houses, and cemeteries. Many families were forced to sell their property to the power company and leave their homes. In some cases, this property had been in the families' hands since before the American Revolution.

Once the basin was cleared of people, it had to be flooded with water from the Housatonic River. Though residents had been relocated, many of the buildings in the valley were left standing. A considerable amount of property, including farm equipment, was left behind. The roads that existed at the time were not torn up before the valley was flooded.

Today, SCUBA divers can journey to the bottom of the lake and follow the old roads underwater. Divers have reported seeing a Model T car, plane wreckage, and covered bridges. They have also discovered portions of farmhouses and their cellars. Candlewood Lake is now a year-round attraction. It is a popular tourist spot for fishing, boating, and golfing. Along its shores are resorts, recreation facilities, beaches, and boat marinas.

With its highest elevation only around 700 feet (213 m), the land slopes downward from northwest to northeast. The Eastern New England Upland stretches from Connecticut to Maine. Most of the Connecticut portion of the Upland is thickly forested.

Part of the Coastal Lowlands that cover the entire coast of New England, the Connecticut Coastal Lowlands form a narrow strip of land 6 to 16 miles (10 to 26 km) wide. It runs

The southern shore of Connecticut borders Long Island Sound. As a result, the coast is dotted with lighthouses, including this one, called Five Mile Point Lighthouse, in New Haven, Connecticut.

along the southern shore of the state at Long Island Sound. Lower than most of Connecticut, the Coastal Lowlands include many beaches, small bays, and inlets along the water.

# Climate

Interior Connecticut is considered to have a humid continental climate. This climate is typical of temperate regions in the midlatitudes, where polar and tropical air masses frequently come into contact. Summers tend to be hot and humid, with frequent and often severe thundershowers, while winters are cold and snowy. Connecticut's shoreline is a humid subtropical climate. Summers are hot and humid, and winters are cool. Significant precipitation falls in all seasons along the coast, usually as rain. The Atlantic Ocean moderates (evens out) temperature extremes somewhat along the coast.

# Plant and Animal Life

Connecticut has a diverse landscape and therefore diverse flora (flowers, plants, and trees) and fauna (animals and birds), too. Along the shore of Long Island Sound are tidal marshes. In and near these marshes are salt grasses, glasswort, purple gerardia, sea lavender, black grass, switchgrass, marsh elder, and sea myrtle. The state's many swamps, bogs, and wetlands are home to ferns, cattails, cranberry, tussock sedge, skunk cabbage, sweet pepperbush, spicebush, and false hellebore. The state's more hilly and mountainous areas include mountain laurel (the state flower), pink azalea, trailing arbutus, Solomon's seal, and Queen Anne's lace.

Before industrial and suburban development, Connecticut provided habitats for bears, wolves, cougars, foxes, panthers, and rattlesnakes. Today, however, the most common animals are woodchucks, squirrels, rabbits, chipmunks, porcupines, raccoons, and skunks. The robin is the state bird. It's joined by blue jays, song sparrows, wood thrushes, and many kinds of waterfowl as the most prevalent bird species in the state.

# Chapter 2

# The History of Connecticut

**Along** the East Coast, just above the sprawling metropolis of New York City, lies a small state that has played a dramatic role in the history of this country. Connecticut is the third smallest state. Though diminutive, it has a rich history of loyalty, patriotism, innovation, industry, and commerce that dates back to its founding as one of the original thirteen colonies of the United States of America.

## European Discovery and Early Settlement

Prior to Connecticut's colonization by European settlers, the Mohegan Indian tribe inhabited the area. Many of the tribe's descendants still live along the upper Thames River Valley.

The first European explorer to discover Connecticut was the Dutchman Adriaen Block. He is credited with being the first European to enter Long Island Sound, navigate the Connecticut River, and recognize that Manhattan and Long Island were islands. Dutch fur traders founded a small fort and settlement in present-day Hartford, but it didn't last very long due to an influx of English settlers nearby.

This illustration shows Thomas Hooker leading his followers from Massachusetts into the wilderness on his way to establishing a colony in Connecticut.

Later, John Winthrop, then of the Massachusetts Bay Colony, received permission in 1635 to create a new colony at Old Saybrook, a settlement located at the mouth of the Connecticut River. At about the same time, Thomas Hooker led a band of followers from Massachusetts and founded what would become the Connecticut Colony. Meanwhile, other settlers from Massachusetts founded the New Haven Colony. These three distinct colonies would later be combined to create the state of Connecticut.

## The Constitution State

The state's official nickname, the Constitution State, was adopted in 1659. The nickname comes from the fact that Connecticut drafted its own constitution, the Fundamental Orders, in 1639, well before the U.S. Constitution was written and adopted. The Fundamental Orders described how the colonial government was set up and run by the Old Saybrook, Connecticut, and New Haven colonies.

This colonial constitution would later influence those who drafted the U.S. Constitution. Roger Sherman, who was from the New Haven Colony and participated in writing the Fundamental Orders, would later assist in shaping the ideals of the federal constitution when the Founding Fathers gathered to write the documents that would define our country's government.

## The American Revolution

During the American Revolution, when the young country was fighting for its independence from the British, Connecticut gave freely in support of the war. Its soldiers were on the battle-fields from Quebec to the Carolinas, and its supplies contributed to the military.

Before the land's colonization by the Europeans, the Mohegan Indian tribe occupied Connecticut. Today, many of the tribe's ancestors still remain in the state.

The city of Danbury became an important military supply depot for the Continental Army, led by General George Washington. On April 26–27, 1777, about two thousand British soldiers landed at the coastal town of Compo Beach in Westport and marched to Danbury. Once there, they burned and looted the city and destroyed colonial army supplies. This resulted in the Battle of Ridgefield, a series of skirmishes fought between Danbury and Compo Beach.

When word of the British troops' movements spread, Connecticut militia leaders sprang into action. They raised a combined force of roughly seven hundred Continental Army soldiers, as well as local militia to fight against the British. They did not reach Danbury in time to save the military supplies or prevent the city from being burned to

# Danbury

In 1685, eight families who had come from elsewhere in Connecticut were the first to settle in Danbury. They initially called the town Swampfield, but it was renamed Danbury two years later. During the American Revolution, it became an important supply depot for the Continental Army. Because of this, the British Army looted and burned the city to the ground in 1777.

After the Revolutionary War, the city was rebuilt and it became a thriving community. In 1780, the city became the world's leading producer of hats. Indeed, Danbury was responsible for as much as 25 percent of the country's headgear. The city was even nicknamed Hat City because of its position as the center of the hat industry.

Beginning in 1821, the city held an annual Danbury Fair, initially an agricultural exposition that evolved into a farmer's market, farm tool and equipment emporium, and carnival of sorts, with rides and attractions. The fair ran until 1981, when the fairgrounds were sold to a developer.

Today, on the site of the old fairgrounds stands the Danbury Fair Mall, the largest shopping mall in Connecticut and the fifth largest in New England. During the summer months, the mall's parking lot is the site of the Danbury City Fair, a minimidway of carnival rides and amusements that provides a nostalgic echo of the former agricultural fair.

Danbury itself continues to echo its own past. Though no longer Hat City, it remains a strong manufacturing city. It is home to several corporate headquarters. These include Ethan Allan Interiors, a furniture company; Scholastic Library Publishing, a leading children's educational publisher; ATMI, a maker of semiconductors and flat panels; and Praxair, a Fortune 500 company that sells industrial gases for use in electronics, metal fabrication, and food processing. No longer a village of eight relocated families, Danbury now has a population of more than seventy-eight thousand. Yet it remains a magnet for those seeking a new home—more than a third of its residents are foreign-born.

the ground. Yet they did set out to harass the redcoats as they marched back to the coast, where a fleet of British ships awaited their return.

# The Industrial Revolution

Following the American Revolution, Connecticut became quite wealthy due to its busy seaports and textile mills. The state was home to a large number of engineers and inventors, such as Eli Whitney. Thanks to their efforts, Connecticut was at the forefront of the next great revolution—the Industrial Revolution. Indeed, Connecticut was issued more patents per capita than any other state for industrial inventions like Whitney's cotton gin and milling machine. Connecticut quickly earned a worldwide reputation for industrial ingenuity.

Whitney and Simeon North began making firearms with interchangeable parts. Eventually, Whitney invented the cotton gin, a manufacturing advancement that sped up the process of cotton refining. The invention also influenced a major movement in the Industrial Revolution in which manufacturing become machine-based. This streamlined processes and improved the speed of production.

Connecticut's industrial might and Whitney's pioneering of interchangeable manufactured machine parts played a huge role in the Civil War. Connecticut was a major supplier of weapons, ammunition, and other materials for the Union Army.

# Connecticut and the Twentieth-Century Defense Industry

Weapons and ammunition manufacturing continued to be an important part of the state economy through World War I and the Great

Hat Factory in Danbury, Conn.

This vintage postcard features an image of one of Danbury's hat factories. Known as Hat City, Danbury at one time produced more than 25 percent of America's hats.

Depression. World War II saw the rise of airplane engine, radio, radar, rifle, parachute, submarine, uniform, and ship manufacturing in Connecticut. During the Cold War years, the Connecticut economy came to rely on the military and defense industries even more.

When the Cold War came to an abrupt end following the fall of Communism and the breakup of the Soviet Union and the Eastern Bloc, Connecticut's economy was forced to diversify. Entertainment (especially casinos owned by the Mashantucket Pequot tribe), tourism, financial services, and pharmaceutical companies began to represent larger pieces of Connecticut's economic pie. Yet manufacturing remains an important and sizable component of Connecticut's economy and employs many of the state's residents.

Through the years, Connecticut's industrial genius has given the world such varied inventions as vulcanized rubber, sewing machines, steamboats, lollipops, corkscrews, mechanical calculators, cylindrical locks, and the submarine. Connecticut is also responsible for major strides in the aviation industry. It's the site of the design and creation of cutting-edge aircraft engines and one of the first powered flights in the country. Not bad for New England's second smallest state!

## Increasing Suburbanization and Diversity

Starting in the 1930s and continuing through the 1960s, a boom in highway construction, including the building of Interstates 95 and 91, resulted in profound changes to Connecticut's landscape and culture. Previously a primarily rural state punctuated by several urban oases, Connecticut soon became dominated by suburbs in the highway era. Many of its new suburban developments served as bedroom communities for commuters who worked in Boston, Providence, or New York. Connecticut's sense of itself as an agricultural producer and an industrial powerhouse began to wane. Farms were sacrificed to suburban sprawl, manufacturing jobs were gradually shed, and cities lost population and wealth to the new housing developments.

Today, Connecticut is a state with a population of roughly 3,510,297. More than 11 percent of the population (four hundred thousand) is foreign-born. The five largest reported ancestries in the state are Italian (18.6 percent), Irish (16.6 percent), English (10.3 percent), German (9.9 percent), and French/French Canadian (9.9 percent).

# Chapter 3

# THE GOVERNMENT OF CONNECTICUT

Connecticut's government structure is the same as that of the U.S. federal government. This means it is composed of three distinct branches—the executive, the legislative, and the judicial. Each of these branches has its own set of powers and responsibilities. The state's capital, Hartford, is where nearly all the state's governmental decisions are made.

Connecticut does have a unique local government structure, called the New England town. This form of government is only practiced in the six states that form the New England region of the United States.

## The Executive Branch

Like every other state in the country, a governor heads the executive branch of Connecticut. The governor presides over several executive departments. These departments cover agriculture, banking, children and families, consumer protection, corrections, economic and community development, education, and environmental protection. They are also concerned with higher education, information technology, insurance, labor, motor vehicles, public health, public safety, social services, transportation, and veterans affairs, among others.

The governor has an extensive staff, including several executive officers, to assist him or her in overseeing the state. These positions include lieutenant governor, secretary of state, treasurer, comptroller, and attorney general. All of these executive branch position holders are elected to office by the voters, and each serves a four-year term.

## The Legislative Branch

Connecticut's legislature is the general assembly, a bicameral (two-chamber) body. The general assembly features an upper body, the state senate, and a lower body, the house of representatives. The state sen-

The Connecticut State Capitol building, located in Hartford, opened in 1878 and became a National Historic Landmark in 1971. The building houses the state's executive offices and legislative chambers.

ate consists of 36 senators, and the house contains 151 representatives. A bill must successfully pass in both the senate and the house in order to become law. The governor can veto a bill, or deny its ability to become a law. However, the governor's veto can be overturned by a two-thirds majority vote in each house. The lieutenant governor presides over the senate. The speaker of the house oversees the house of representatives.

# The New England Town

The New England town is the most basic unit of local government in New England. Incorporating territory into towns dates back to the time of the earliest European colonial settlement of New England.

Throughout the seventeenth, eighteenth, and nineteenth centuries, areas were organized into towns as they were settled. Usually, large areas of land were organized within a town designation. Once these large areas became settled and more densely populated, they would often be broken up into several smaller towns. Each town was governed by the unique New England town meeting system, in which regular citizens gather to debate and decide on legislative matters.

Towns were long the main, if not the only, form of municipality in New England. So even Boston, the largest population center in New England, remained a town for its first two hundred years before finally being designated a city. By the end of the 1700s, all of Connecticut's territory had been incorporated into towns. That means every square foot of territory belongs within one town or another.

Today, more than 90 percent of all municipalities in New England are still designated as towns. Local town government remains strong. In fact, the town government enjoys all the powers that city governments do in other states. County governments, which usually dominate local politics in other states, are weak throughout New England. In fact, there is no county government in Connecticut. While the state is divided into counties, these divisions are used largely for geographical and statistical purposes, such as weather and census reporting.

Connecticut is divided into 169 towns. The twenty-one cities in Connecticut have all grown from smaller towns over a few hundred years. Each city is classified as both a city and a town, and each shares a merged city-town government. Some Connecticut towns are large enough to qualify as cities, yet cling to their town designation. With these large towns, the town hall form of government often takes on more citylike forms, with town meetings conducted by elected representatives and town managers.

Like every other state, Connecticut has two U.S. senators. The state also has five representatives in the U.S. House of Representatives.

## The Judicial Branch

The highest court of the state judicial branch is the Connecticut Supreme Court. Headed by the chief justice of Connecticut, the Supreme Court is responsible for deciding on the

The Connecticut State Supreme Court building, located in downtown Hartford, is the center of justice where state laws are upheld.

constitutionality of state law and judging cases as they relate to state law. Its proceedings are similar to those of the U.S. Supreme Court. Following a court proceeding, the court may take several months to arrive at a judgment.

The superior courts are lower courts that resemble the county courts of other states. The appellate court hears appeals to these lower courts' decisions.

# Chapter 4

# THE ECONOMY OF CONNECTICUT

**Connecticut** has long held a prominent place in aviation history as a state that has fostered the invention and manufacturing of aircraft and aircraft parts. However, its role as a leading industrial manufacturer is not limited to just aviation. Transportation has been a large state industry, as has the building of nuclear submarines, helicopters, military weaponry, and scientific products.

As one of the nation's most industrialized, technologically advanced, and prosperous states, Connecticut has excelled in a wide range of industries that drive its economy. Modern areas of excellence include financial services (especially the insurance industry based in Hartford), health and biomedical services, business services, and entertainment (especially Native American–owned casinos). Other major Connecticut industries include advanced manufacturing, education, research and development, tourism, transportation, agriculture, and forestry and fishing.

## Advanced Manufacturing

Connecticut has been the location for major industrial inventions and creations. The state is home to many firsts: the first published

A pioneer in the history of aviation, Connecticut is also a leader in the manufacturing of helicopters and aircraft parts. Sikorsky Aircraft, based in Connecticut, built this CH-53E helicopter.

newspaper (1764), the first hamburger (1895), the Polaroid camera (1934), the helicopter (1939), and color television (1948). Today, most of the state's manufacturing industries are concentrated in Fairfield, Hartford, and New Haven counties. The cities of Hartford, Bridgeport, New Haven, New Britain, Waterbury, Stamford, and Norwalk are leading manufacturing centers. Among the companies that have headquarters in Connecticut are Time Warner Cable, Pitney Bowes (software, marketing, and business services), Xerox Corporation, International Paper, General Electric, and Thomson Corporation (a provider of business information).

## Mystic Seaport

Since the 1600s, the banks of the Mystic River have been the center of shipbuilding in Connecticut. In a 135-year period stretching from the eighteenth to the twentieth centuries, more than 600 wooden sailing ships were constructed there. With the arrival of the Industrial Revolution and steam-powered ships, however, traditional wooden shipbuilding went into decline. Mystic soon became known more for its textile manufacturing than its shipbuilding.

With the decline in Mystic's shipbuilding fortunes, Connecticut's rich maritime heritage became endangered. In an attempt to prevent the disappearance of the state's seafaring traditions, three men—a doctor, lawyer, and merchant with seafaring experience and family histories of shipbuilding—banded together to restore Mystic's stature in the public consciousness. Together, they formed the Marine Historical Association in 1929. Through the association, they hoped to create an educational institute that would celebrate and preserve Connecticut's—and America's—maritime culture and history.

The form this institution took was the Mystic Seaport. Initially, it was a small museum stocked with donated ship's logbooks, photographs, blueprints, and other maritime artifacts. Then the museum began to expand with the acquisition of various historic buildings and an authentic whaling ship. The result was the creation of a period-appropriate shipbuilding and whaling village, a sort of living museum of maritime culture.

Today, the Mystic Seaport contains the world's largest collections of maritime photography (more than one million images) and boats (nearly five hundred). It also boasts more than two million other maritime artifacts, the Henry B. duPont Preservation Shipyard, additional exhibition buildings, the Collections Research Center, and several accredited educational programs. The seaport is the nation's largest maritime museum with three hundred thousand yearly visitors, twenty-five thousand members, and three hundred employees.

# Education, Research, and Development

Yale University is one of the largest employers in the state, with nearly thirteen thousand faculty and staff, and its research activity has generated dozens of new biotechnology companies. The influence of Yale and its faculty of leading experts, academics, researchers, and scientists has also benefitted the larger community and

Yale University, located in New Haven, is one of America's oldest universities. Each year more than eleven thousand students study at this Ivy League school.

local economy. The city of New Haven, where Yale is located, has become the world's leading center for life sciences research. Discoveries in Yale laboratories have led to more than forty start-up companies in the Greater New Haven area. Their work centers on biological discoveries, biotechnology, genetic engineering, and biological chemistry.

Connecticut has other well-known and respected colleges and universities. These include Trinity College, Wesleyan University, the University of Hartford, the U.S. Coast Guard Academy, and Quinnipiac University. Also notable for excellence is the Connecticut State University System, which includes the University of Connecticut, also known as UConn. According to *U.S. News & World Report*, UConn has been the highest-ranked public university in New England throughout the 2000s.

# Tourism

Many visitors are attracted to Connecticut for its beautiful landscape, which includes rolling green hills, lakes, and beautifully preserved colonial-era towns and villages. The north shore of Long Island Sound and Litchfield Hills are among the major resort areas in the state. Connecticut maintains a system of more than fifty state parks. The most popular of these include Gillette Castle State Park in Haddam, Hammonassett Beach State Park in Madison, Sherwood Island State Park in Westport, and Dinosaur State Park in Rocky Hill. Connecticut is also a popular ski destination, with several major ski resorts welcoming skiers, snowboarders, and snowshoe enthusiasts in the winter. Among Connecticut's most popular tourist attractions are Mystic Seaport, Dinosaur State Park, the Wadsworth Atheneum, the Goodspeed Opera House, and the home of author Mark Twain.

# Transportation

Connecticut's transportation system is highly developed. The state has about 20,850 miles (33,555 km) of roads and highways that allow commuters to get to their destinations. The state also operates more than 580 miles (933 km) of railroad track, which serve many of the residents who work in neighboring New York City. One major commuter rail line with several spurs brings commuters from as far away as New Haven, Danbury, and Waterbury into midtown Manhattan. Amtrak has two major rail lines running through the state. Connecticut also has fifty-four airports, ninety-two heliports, and five seaplane bases. The state's busiest air terminal is Bradley International Airport in Windsor Locks. New

The Metro-North Commuter Railroad offers daily service between New York City and various points in Connecticut, making commuting into the city for work and pleasure fairly quick and easy.

Haven, Bridgeport, and New London have port facilities that manage a large amount of freight shipped around the world. A year-round ferry service also connects Connecticut to Long Island via Long Island Sound.

## Agriculture

While not the largest industry in Connecticut, farming does produce a fair amount of agricultural products and revenue each year. Greenhouse and nursery products, such as flowers and shrubs for landscaping, make up the majority of the state's agriculture. Dairy products, chickens, eggs, beef cattle, tobacco, sweet corn, apples, hay, and peaches generate much of the rest of the state's agricultural income.

One area of agricultural growth that is just beginning to hit its stride is the wine industry. In 1978, Connecticut passed the Connecticut Winery Act. This piece of legislation made it legal for wine to be produced commercially in the state. Since then, more than sixteen wineries have been established throughout the state. Connecticut wines have begun to earn an international reputation for their quality.

## Forestry and Fishing

Forestry activities used to be big business in Connecticut. Now that much of the state's timber has been depleted, very little commercial forestry exists in the state.

Fishing also represents a small and dwindling portion of the state's economy. Oysters and hard-shell clams are harvested along Long Island Sound. Fishermen catch flounder, cod, menhaden, porgy, whiting, and lobster and sell the fish for profit.

# Chapter 5

# PEOPLE FROM CONNECTICUT: PAST AND PRESENT

**There** have been many famous actors and actresses, political leaders, musicians and singers, literary greats, and captains of industry who have called Connecticut home. Those that follow are just a few.

## Political and Military Leaders

**Benedict Arnold (1741–1801)** Benedict Arnold, born and raised in Norwich, served as a general of the Continental Army during the American Revolution. Though a brilliant and effective general in the early days of the war, Arnold eventually became notorious for betraying the cause and switching to the British side. As a result, his name has become synonymous with "traitor."

**Ralph Nader (1934– )** Ralph Nader is an attorney, author, and political activist who ran for president of the United States in 2000, 2004, and 2008. Born and raised in Winsted, Nader is an expert in consumer protection, humanitarianism, and environmentalism. He supports liberal democratic causes and governmental policies.

P. T. Barnum was an author, publisher, philanthropist, and politician. However, his greatest success was as a founder of the Ringling Bros. and Barnum & Bailey Circus.

**Roger Sherman (1721–1793)** Roger Sherman is the only person to sign all four of the United States' most important founding documents: the Continental Association (a 1774 agreement drafted by the First Continental Congress that declared a boycott against trade with Great Britain), the Declaration of Independence, the Articles of Confederation, and the U.S. Constitution. Sherman also served as the first mayor of New Haven.

## Captains of Industry

### P. T. Barnum (1810–1891)

Bethel native P. T. Barnum was a businessman and entertainer. He founded the circus that eventually became the world-renown Ringling Bros. and Barnum & Bailey Circus. His success made him one of the first show business millionaires. Barnum was the first circus owner to move his entire circus, including his performers and animals, by train. At the time, there were very few paved highways in America, so travel by train enabled Barnum to reach communities throughout the country with his traveling circus.

**Edwin H. Land (1909– 1991)** Born in Bridgeport, Edwin H. Land cofounded the Polaroid Corporation and invented the Polaroid camera, which produced instant photographs with film that did not require processing. Land was also famous for helping to design a revolutionary spy plane, the Lockheed U-2. This plane provided the U.S. government with highly detailed surveillance during daytime and nighttime missions.

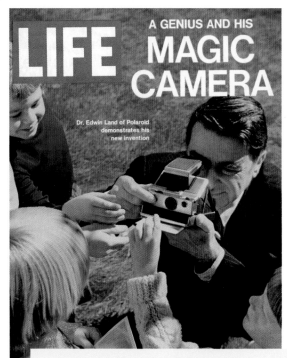

Famous for instantly capturing an image and printing the picture within seconds, Edwin Land's Polaroid camera was first introduced to the public in 1948 and became a huge success.

**Eli Whitney (1765–1825)**

Yale graduate and New Haven resident Eli Whitney invented the cotton gin, one of the key inventions of the Industrial Revolution. His machine, which removed seeds from cotton, made cotton harvesting much more efficient. Until his invention, slaves and laborers removed the seeds by hand, which was time-consuming and physically exhausting. His invention helped fuel the manufacturing industry in America,

## Yale

Yale University, an Ivy League school that is one of the most famous centers of learning, has humble beginnings. At the direction of the Colony of Connecticut, the Collegiate School (as it was first called) was founded in 1701 with the purpose of training ministers and religious leaders. Its first library was formed by books donated by ten ministers who had all attended Harvard University. These men became known as the Founders. The school was first located in Killingworth (present-day Clinton). It then moved to Saybrook and Wethersfield before settling permanently in New Haven.

Father and son Puritan ministers Increase and Cotton Mather, who had split from Harvard, fostered the Collegiate School's success. They believed that Harvard was sliding away from strict Puritan principles, and so they threw all of their considerable influence behind the new Collegiate School. To increase the school's fortunes, they sought and received financial investment from a wealthy Welsh businessman, Elihu Yale, whose donations of goods and books propelled the school into Harvard's rank. The school was renamed in his honor. Thus was born the longstanding and bitter rivalry between Harvard and Yale.

Today, Yale is the third-oldest institution of higher education in the country, behind only Harvard University (founded in 1636) and the College of William and Mary (1693). It has two dozen libraries, twelve residential colleges, and numerous schools, such as the School of Medicine, the School of Divinity, and the School of Drama. It has an endowment (a collection of donations for the purpose of investment in the university's operations and development) worth several billion dollars.

Yale has produced many notable alumni. This illustrious roster includes five U.S. presidents (William Howard Taft, Gerald Ford, George H. W. Bush, William Clinton, and George W. Bush), nineteen U.S. Supreme Court justices (including Samuel Alito, Sonia Sotomayor, and Clarence Thomas), and several foreign heads of state. Its School of Drama has produced many talented actors, including Paul Newman, Meryl Streep, Jodie Foster, and Claire Danes.

which would be driven by power machinery and inter-changeable parts.

## Literary Greats

**Harriet Beecher Stowe (1811–1896)** Harriet Beecher Stowe's novel *Uncle Tom's Cabin*, which depicts the harsh life of African American slaves, is considered one of the most important spurs to antislavery sentiment and the resulting Civil War. The book rallied support for the cause of abolition (ending slavery), especially among residents of states in the North. As a result, Stowe, who was born in Litchfield and died in Hartford, enraged slave owners in the South.

**Mark Twain (1835–1910)** Mark Twain, whose real name was Samuel Clemens, lived in Hartford when he wrote *The Adventures of Tom Sawyer*. His second novel, *The Adventures of Huckleberry Finn*, has been called the first great American novel. These books would become two of the most famous works in American and world literature. Twain also wrote *A Connecticut Yankee in King Arthur's Court*, a novel about a nineteenth-century Hartford resident who wakes up one morning in medieval England, magically transported across time and space to Camelot.

## Entertainment

**Katherine Hepburn (1907–2003)** Katherine Hepburn is a four-time Academy Award winner who holds the record for winning the most Oscars in the Best Actress category.

Grammy Award–winning musician John Mayer was born and raised in Connecticut. *Rolling Stone* magazine named Mayer one of the one hundred greatest guitarists of all time.

Hepburn's most famous films are *Morning Glory*, *Bringing Up Baby*, *The Philadelphia Story*, *Adam's Rib*, *Woman of the Year*, *The African Queen*, *Lion in Winter*, *Guess Who's Coming to Dinner*, and *On Golden Pond*. She was born in Hartford and was a longtime resident of Old Saybrook, where she died in 2003.

**John Mayer (1977– )** Bridgeport native John Mayer is a Grammy Award–winning musician and singer whose four albums have sold more than ten million copies. He is among the finest guitarists of his generation. Mayer considers himself a guitarist first and a singer-songwriter second.

**Meryl Streep (1949– )** Meryl Steep is a two-time Oscar winning–actress and is the most nominated individual in the history of the Academy Awards. Streep has been nominated a record fifteen times! She has appeared in more than sixty films, including the hit comedy *It's Complicated* (2009), co-starring Steve Martin and Alec Baldwin. She is a graduate of the Yale School of Drama and makes her home in Connecticut.

# Timeline

|  |  |
|---|---|
| **1614** | The first European settlers land on Connecticut's shores and sail up the Connecticut River. |
| **1636** | One of the most famous early Connecticut settlers, Reverend Thomas Hooker, travels from Massachusetts with a group of colonists. They found the town of Hartford. Eventually, Hartford, Wethersfield, and Windsor become the Connecticut Colony. |
| **1639** | Thomas Hooker, John Haynes, and Roger Ludlow write a document called the Fundamental Orders of Connecticut, the first written constitution. Many historians have said that this document served as the basis for the U.S. Constitution. |
| **1701** | Yale University is founded. It is originally known as the Collegiate School. |
| **1764** | Thomas Green launches the *Connecticut Courant*, the oldest American newspaper in continuous existence. It is still in operation today. |
| **1788** | Connecticut becomes the fifth state of the United States of America. |
| **1792** | Eli Whitney develops the cotton gin in New Haven. |
| **1837** | The first railroad begins service in Connecticut. |
| **1845** | Elias Howe invents the sewing machine. |
| **1875** | Hartford becomes Connecticut's capital. |
| **1877** | The first telephone exchange in the world is opened in New Haven. |
| **1954** | The first atomic submarine, the *Nautilus*, is launched at Groton. |
| **1958** | The Connecticut Turnpike (I-95), a 129-mile (208 km) route that runs east and west across the state, opens. |
| **1974** | Ella Grasso is elected the first female governor of Connecticut. |
| **1979** | Connecticut passes a law banning the construction of nuclear power plants. |
| **2009** | For the second year in a row, Connecticut College ranks among the top twenty colleges nationwide for media presence. |

# Connecticut at a Glance

| | |
|---|---|
| **State motto:** | *Qui transtulit sustinet* ("He who is transplanted sustains") |
| **State capital:** | Hartford |
| **State flower:** | Mountain laurel |
| **State tree:** | Charter white oak |
| **State bird:** | American robin |
| **State animal:** | Sperm whale |
| **Statehood date and number:** | January 5, 1788; fifth state |
| **State nicknames:** | Constitution State and Nutmeg State |
| **Total area and U.S. rank:** | 5,543 square miles (14,356 sq km); forty-eighth largest state |
| **Population:** | 3,501,000 |
| **Length of coastline:** | 96 miles (154.5 km) |
| **Highest elevation:** | South slope of Mount Frissell, at 2,380 feet (725 m) |
| **Lowest elevation:** | Long Island Sound, at 0 feet (0 m) |
| **Major rivers:** | Connecticut River, Housatonic River, Thames River |

State Flag

State Seal

| | |
|---|---|
| **Major lake:** | Candlewood Lake |
| **Highest recorded temperature:** | 106 degrees Fahrenheit (41.1 degrees Celsius) in Danbury, July 15, 1995 |
| **Lowest recorded temperature:** | -32°F (-35.6°C) in Coventry, January 22, 1961 |
| **Origin of state name:** | The name "Connecticut" originates from the Mohegan Indian word *quinnitukqut*, which means "place of long tidal river" |
| **Chief agricultural products:** | Eggs, dairy products, chickens, beef cattle, sweet corn, apples, hay, peaches, tobacco, flounder, cod, menhaden, porgy, whiting, clams, lobster, oysters |
| **Major industries:** | Aircraft/aviation, aircraft parts, nuclear submarines, military weaponry, transportation and transportation equipment, scientific instruments, financial services, health and biomedical services, business services, entertainment, advanced manufacturing, biotechnology, computer software, education, research, and development, tourism, agriculture, forestry, fishing |

American robin

Mountain laurel

**aviation** The operation of aircraft.

**biotechnology** The application of biology and technology to bring about medical breakthroughs.

**colony** A distant territory that is owned by a parent nation.

**constitution** The basic principles and laws of a nation, state, or social group that determine the powers and duties of the government and guarantee certain rights to the people under that government.

**Continental Army** A military group composed of rebellious colonists formed during the American Revolution.

**county** A large land area within a state encompassing several villages, towns, and perhaps a city. It often features its own government.

**genetic engineering** Applied techniques of genetics and biotechnology used to separate and join genetic material from one or more species of organism in order to introduce the material to another organism to change its characteristics.

**greenhouse** An enclosed structure used for growing plants, flowers, and vegetation.

**inlet** A bay or recess in the shore of a sea, lake, or river.

**Ivy League** A group of eight long-established eastern colleges and universities widely regarded as occupying the top positions in scholastic and social prestige.

**lowlands** A geographic landscape located at or below sea level.

**metropolis** A greater urban area that includes a city and its suburbs.

**militia** Part of the organized armed forces of a country that can be called upon in an emergency.

**Model T** Regarded as the first affordable automobile, the Model T was designed and built by the Ford Motor Company.

**upland** Land located at a high elevation, often some distance from the sea or ocean.

**veto** The power of one government entity to forbid the carrying out of projects, laws, or rules proposed by another entity.

## Audubon Connecticut

613 Riversville Road

Greenwich, CT 06831

(203) 869-5272

Web site: http://www.audubonct.org

Audubon Connecticut is the state office of the National Audubon Society. Its mission is to further the protection of birds, other wildlife, and their habitats through science, education, advocacy, and conservation.

## Connecticut Commission on Culture and Tourism

One Constitution Plaza, 2nd Floor

Hartford, CT 06103

1-888-CTvisit [280-6103]

Web site: http://www.ctvisit.com

The mission of the commission is to preserve and promote Connecticut's cultural and tourism assets in order to enhance the quality of life and economic vitality of the state.

## Connecticut Historical Society

One Elizabeth Street at Asylum Avenue

Hartford, CT 06105

(860) 236-5621

Web site: http://www.chs.org

This nonprofit, which consists of a museum, library, and education center, seeks to foster a lifelong interest in history through exhibitions, programs, and Connecticut-related collections.

## Connecticut State Capitol

210 Capitol Avenue

Hartford, CT 06106

Web site: http://www.ct.gov

The Connecticut State Capitol Web site is the official government Web site for the state of Connecticut.

## Connecticut State Library

231 Capitol Avenue

Hartford, CT 06106

(860) 757-6500

Web site: http://www.cslib.org

The library provides various information and administrative services for citizens of Connecticut, as well as for government employees and officials.

## ConneCT Kids

111 Phoenix Avenue

Enfield, CT 06082

(860) 741-3027

Web site: http://www.kids.ct.gov/kids/site/default.asp

The ConneCT Kids Web site highlights Connecticut history, government, state symbols, and more.

## Museum of Connecticut History

231 Capitol Avenue

Hartford, CT 06106

(860) 757-6535

Web site: http://www.museumofcthistory.org

The museum focuses on Connecticut's government, military, and industrial history. Exhibits trace the growth of the state and its role in the development of the nation.

## University of Connecticut

Storrs, CT 06269

(860) 486-2000

Web site: http://www.uconn.edu

Ranked the top public university in New England, the University of Connecticut is among the best public institutions in the country.

## Yale University Mead Visitor Center

149 Elm Street

New Haven, CT 06511

(203) 432-2300

Web site: http://www.yale.edu/visitor

The Mead Visitor Center welcomes visitors from around the world to Yale University. Regularly scheduled tours are free of charge and do not require an appointment.

# Web Sites

Due to the changing nature of Internet links, Rosen Publishing has developed an online list of Web sites related to the subject of this book. This site is updated regularly. Please use this link to access the list:

http://www.rosenlinks.com/uspp/ctpp

# FOR FURTHER READING

Burgan, Michael. *Connecticut 1614–1776* (Voices from Colonial America). Washington, DC: National Geographic Children's Books, 2007.

Campbell, Susan, and Bill Heald. *Connecticut Curiosities: Quirky Characters, Roadside Oddities & Other Offbeat Stuff.* 2nd ed. Guilford, CT: Globe Pequot Press, 2006.

Dubois, Muriel L. *The Connecticut Colony.* Mankato, MN: Capstone Press, 2006.

Evento, Susan. *Connecticut* (Rookie Read-About Geography). New York, NY: Children's Press, 2005.

Furstinger, Nancy. *Connecticut* (From Sea to Shining Sea). Danbury, CT: Children's Press, 2008.

Kent, Donna. *Ghost Stories and Legends of Eastern Connecticut: Lore, Mysteries, and Secrets Revealed.* Salem, MA: The History Press, 2007.

Kent, Zachary. *Connecticut* (America the Beautiful). New York, NY: Children's Press, 2008.

Labairon, Cassandra. *Connecticut* (This Land Called America). Mankato, MN: Creative Education, 2008.

Laschever, Barnett D., and Andi Marie Cantele. *Connecticut: An Explorer's Guide.* Woodstock, VT: The Countryman Press, 2006.

Lehman, Eric D. *Bridgeport: Tales from the Park City.* Salem, MA: The History Press, 2009.

Malaspina, Ann. A *Primary Source History of the Colony of Connecticut* (Primary Sources of the Thirteen Colonies and the Lost Colony). New York, NY: Rosen Publishing Group, 2005.

McCain, Diana Ross. *Connecticut Coast: A Town-by-Town Illustrated History.* Guilford, CT: Globe Pequot Press, 2009.

Monagan, Charles. *Connecticut Icons: 50 Symbols of the Nutmeg State.* Guilford, CT: Globe Pequot Press, 2006.

Petrlik Smolik, Jane. *The Great Connecticut Puzzle Book.* Wenham, MA: MidRun Press, 2006.

Rothman, Sam. *Historic Photos of Connecticut.* Nashville, TN: Turner Publishing, 2008.

# BIBLIOGRAPHY

Candlewood Lake. "Welcome to Candlewood Lake." Retrieved November 22, 2009
     (http://www.candlewoodlake.org).

City-Data. "Connecticut Industry." Retrieved November 22, 2009 (http://www.city-data.
     com/states/Connecticut-Industry.html).

Connecticut History Online. "Homepage." Retrieved November 15, 2009 (http://www.
     cthistoryonline.org).

ConneCT Kids. "Connecticut History." Retrieved November 22, 2009 (http://www.kids.
     ct.gov/kids/site/default.asp).

McCain, Diana Ross. *Connecticut Coast: A Town-by-Town Illustrated History*. Guilford, CT:
     Globe Pequot Press, 2009.

McCain, Diana Ross. *It Happened in Connecticut*. Guilford, CT: Globe Pequot Press, 2008.

Museum of Connecticut History. "Connecticut Invents!" Retrieved November 15, 2009
     (http://ctinventor.wordpress.com).

Roth, David M. *Connecticut: A History*. New York, NY: W. W. Norton & Co., 1979.

SHG Resources. "Guide to Connecticut History." Retrieved November 15, 2009
     (http://www.shgresources.com/ct/history).

Things To Do. "State Facts: Connecticut." Retrieved November 15, 2009
     (http://www.thingstodo.com/states/CT/facts.htm).

World Almanac for Kids. "Connecticut." Retrieved November 22, 2009 (http://www.
     worldalmanacforkids.com/WAKI-ViewArticle.aspx?pin = wwwwak-368&article_
     id = 745&chapter_id = 15&chapter_title = United_States&article_title =
     Connecticut).

Yale University. "About Yale and New Haven." Retrieved November 22, 2009 (http://
     www.yale.edu/onhsa/index.htm).

## About the Author

Laura La Bella is the author of more than a dozen nonfiction children's books devoted to American history, industry, society, and culture, among other topics. She has relatives who immigrated to Connecticut from Eastern Europe early in the twentieth century. La Bella is a graduate of St. John Fisher College and Rochester Institute of Technology. She lives in Rochester, New York, with her husband.

## Photo Credits

Cover (top left) Library of Congress Prints and Photographs Division; cover (top right) © www.istockphoto.com/Kenneth Wiedemann; cover (bottom) © www.istockphoto.com/Orest Ladyshynsky; pp. 3, 6, 13, 20, 24, 31, 38 © www.istockphoto.com/William Britten; p. 4 © GeoAtlas; p. 7 © www.istockphoto.com/Vivek Nigam; pp. 8, 25, 29 © AP Images; pp. 11, 21 © www.istockphoto.com/Dennis Jr. Tangney; p. 14 Private Collection/Peter Newark American Pictures/Bridgeman Art Library; p. 15 Smithsonian American Art Museum, Washington, DC/Art Resource, NY; p. 18 Wikipedia; p. 23 © www.istockphoto.com/Natalia Bratslavsky; pp. 27, 40 Shutterstock.com; p. 32 Hulton Archive/Getty Images; p. 33 Co Rentmeester/Life Magazine/Time & Life Pictures/Getty Images; p. 36 Valerie Macon/AFP/Getty Images; p. 39 (left) Courtesy of Robesus, Inc.

Designer: Les Kanturek; Photo Researcher: Amy Feinberg